LEAD MINING
IN
SW[illegible]

From [illegible]
Edward R. Fawcett, edited by Brian Lee.

Published by Faust Publishing Co. Ltd.
Thorneyholme Hall
Roughlee
Burnley BB12 9LH

Printed by Flaydemouse
2 Church St., Merriott, Somerset TA16 5PR

ISBN: 0 948558 00 8

Cover - Old Gang Smelt Mills

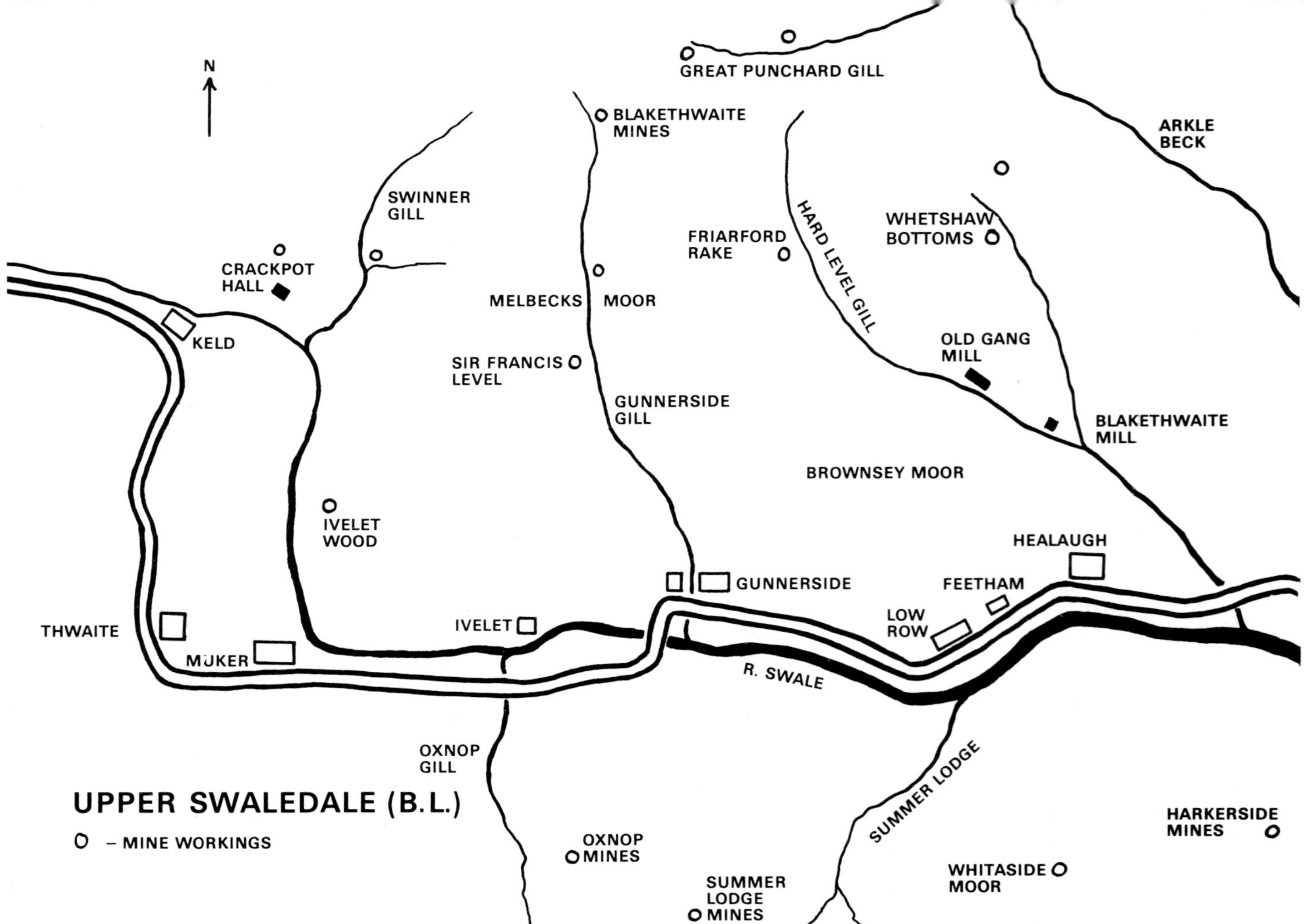
N
GREAT PUNCHARD GILL
BLAKETHWAITE MINES
ARKLE BECK
SWINNER GILL
WHETSHAW BOTTOMS
FRIARFORD RAKE
HARD LEVEL GILL
CRACKPOT HALL
MELBECKS MOOR
KELD
OLD GANG MILL
SIR FRANCIS LEVEL
GUNNERSIDE GILL
BLAKETHWAITE MILL
BROWNSEY MOOR
IVELET WOOD
HEALAUGH
GUNNERSIDE
FEETHAM
THWAITE
IVELET
LOW ROW
MUKER
R. SWALE
OXNOP GILL
SUMMER LODGE
UPPER SWALEDALE (B.L.)
O – MINE WORKINGS
OXNOP MINES
HARKERSIDE MINES
WHITASIDE MOOR
SUMMER LODGE MINES

Foreword

The Swaledale lead industry began to decline in the final quarter of the 19th century.

Cheap imports of foreign lead caused its demise. A tradition of lead mining going back to Celtic times was ended. By the early twentieth century all the large mines had closed and, except for a few small exceptions, the mines have remained closed to the present day.

The redundant miners attempted to find new outlets for their skills. Some moved to the Durham and Northumberland coal mines. Others migrated to Lancashire. They found work in the Lancashire coal mines and their wives and families were employed in the cotton mills. This opportunity of work, often with better pay and conditions, soon depopulated a once thriving dale. Many Swaledale people never returned.

Edward R. Fawcett's father was one of the lead miners who was no longer able to find work. He took his family to the Burnley coalfield area of Lancashire. Edward was ten years old at the time and would have had little opportunity to continue his elementary education. But he was a keen student and later took advantage of the evening classes which were provided in the local Mechanics' Institute. Philip Snowden, who later became Chancellor of the Exchequer, was a fellow student and life-long friend. As a result of his endeavours Edward gained a scholarship to the university at South Kensington. Unfortunately he could not afford to go, but his talents were not wasted as he became a part time teacher of Geology, Physiology, Astronomy and Hygiene.

With the rise in lead prices caused by the First World War he was able to return to Swaledale where he formed a partnership to work the mines at Arngill and Ivelet in the upper dale. As the war ended the venture came to an end but Edward Fawcett was able to stay in the dale, supported by his draper business.

Throughout his life he was fascinated by the history of Swaledale mining. He collected stories of the mining days and painstakingly searched through historic documents to build up a detailed picture of the lead trade. His manuscript has provided inspiration and source material for several well-known chroniclers of dales life. There was a move to publish the manuscript but, with the outbreak of hostilities and the writer's death in 1939, this project never came to fruition.

However, the manuscript has been carefully preserved by its author's grand-daughter – Miriam Wright – who has kindly made it available for publication in its present form.

To fit the space available much editing, re-ordering and linking has been required. Hopefully, the joins will not be too obvious. I have attempted to concentrate on an overall scenario of the development of the lead industry and its techniques rather than including a lot of specific detail about the many individual mines and companies. The Pomfret versus Smith law-suit is only briefly referred to although it occupies many pages of the original manuscript. Stories of human interest have been retained in order to concentrate on the aspects of tenacity and frugality which were characteristics of Swaledale's inhabitants.

In a letter to Edward Fawcett, of December 1927, the naturalist Richard Kearton writes of the Swaledale people:

"The faith and sterling qualities of our forefathers in Swaledale were beyond price. Oh, that some man would arise gifted enough to give full praise to the heroes of sixty or seventy years ago. When I think of the undaunted spirits, who tramped the hillsides day and night to and from their work – work hard, hazardous and ill paid – in all sorts of foul weather whilst their wives, brave souls, stayed at home and with loving care, minded the few acres of dear land and uncomfortable homes. I am filled with a burning admiration. Courageous hearts, you were surely the salt of this God's earth of ours, and my eternal regret is, that I have neither the knowledge nor the strength to record your deeds in words of fire, as I should love to do.

"Anyway I take my hat off to the humblest of you, and say, thank God for your example.

"Oh, if the young people of Swaledale, could only have some admiration for their splendid forebears instilled into them, however proud it would make them feel."

It is the editor's opinion that Edward Fawcett has accomplished that task.

Brian H. Lee

Historical Background

Lead mining in Swaledale dates back to at least the Roman occupation of Britain, as evidenced by the number of pigs of lead found in various parts of the kingdom, bearing the name of many of the Roman Emperors.

It is very probable that the Roman camp at Bainbridge may have served as a centre for the lead trade in the surrounding dales from which men were sent into Swaledale to mine for lead.

Tradition relates that Hurst Mines in Swaledale was one of the Roman penal settlements where convicts were sent to work, and that buildings in Jerusalem and St Peter's in Rome were roofed with lead obtained from the Hurst Mines. Residents of Hurst can still show us an iron ring, leaded into the rock, to which prisoners were chained for misdemeanour.

After the Roman occupation of Britain, which ended in the early part of the year 410 AD, the country was invaded by the Anglo Saxons, many of whom settled in England. Afterwards came Scandinavians and Danes. They pushed their way inland, from both the East and West coasts of England, and formed settlements in many districts. To the Scandinavians, Swaledale owes many of its place names and dialect.

The fact that these invaders settled in such a wild desolate moorland district as Swaledale – when much more congenial districts could have been occupied – points to their chief objective being the rich deposits of lead ore existing in the dale. They, of necessity, cultivated the land, built many of the villages and carried on a trade in lead, much in the same way as the Romans when Catterick was the trading capital of the dale.

The Venerable Bede, 672 AD, relates that merchants visited Catterick to bargain with the Swaledale miners for lead.

The land in Swaledale has been cultivated from very early times, much earlier in fact that in many more fertile districts where the land was more easily reclaimed from nature.

This fact leads the writer to infer that the settlers who first inhabited and cultivated the dale had as their first objective the winning of the rich lead deposits. The cultivation of the land was to them a secondary consideration, yet one which had to be undertaken to provide the necessities of life.

After the Norman Conquest in 1066 AD many valuable records were kept and handed down by the landed gentry who benefited by grants of land leased to them by the King for services rendered during the Conquest. In many of the records reference is made to the lead mines in various districts.

In the Articles of the Ancient use of Tenant Right and Custom in

Swaledale, the 11th item reads:– "Item, that when any Lead Mines shall happen to be found within the Lordship, the finder thereof is to have the same, according to the law and custom of Mines there."

This right must have been taken from the miners some time after the Norman Conquest because, after that date, frequent references are made in old indentures and decrees to the rights to all mines being vested in the Lord of the manor.

At the time of the Norman Conquest Swaledale belonged to Edwyn, Earl of Mercia. He was allowed by William to retain his possessions.

Several years afterwards, Edwyn started a revolt against the King, who granted his lands in Yorkshire to his nephew Alan, Earl of Bretagne, in the following words:– I William Surnamed the Bastard, do give and grant to thee Alan my nephew Earl of Bretagne and to thy heirs forever, all the towns and lands which lately belonged to Earl Edwyn, in Yorkshire, with the Knights Fees, churches, and other privileges and customs, in as free and honourable manner as the said Edwyn held them. Given from the siege of York.

Bodin, in 1096, held the Manors of Grinton and Reeth (Dom Bk Fac 27) and one of his descendants, Brian, son of Alan, claimed half the forest of Swaledale in 1207–8.

The lands in Swaledale were granted to Walter de Gaunt, a relative of William the Conqueror, on his marriage to the Earl of Richmond's daughter, Maud, 1094 AD. He also succeeded to Folkingham in Lincolnshire, the family seat of the Gaunts, and inherited the estates of his father, Gilbert. In addition to building Grinton Church he founded Bridlington Priory. He died in 1138 or 1139 AD (GEC peerage v 88).

Walter distinguished himself at the battle of the Standard, and according to the Ballad of Cowton Moor, the king asked:

"Who is yon chiefe, that rydes along
With hys lockes soe aged grey?" He was told:
"Oh that is Walter de Gawnte you see
And he hath beene greye full long.
But many's the troope that he dothe leade
And they are stoute and Stronge."

(Ingledew ballads and songs of Yorks 21)

Walter de Gaunt's descendants held lands in Swaledale on payment of four knights' fees at Richmond Castle, free of ward, but paying a pair of gilt spurs yearly. (Gales Reg Hist. de Richmond.)

At the death of Walter de Gaunt his lands descended to his son Gilbert de Gaunt who died 1274 AD. (Inquisition Post Mortem 2 Edward I.) At Gilbert's death his estates were inherited by his son, Gilbert the second. Gilbert de Gaunt held the Manor of Healaugh in Swaledale from the Lord John Brittania, Earl of Richmond, 1268 by the service of one pair of gilt spurs by the year, for all service. He also held the Manor of Muker and Grinton. We find that in the year 1312, at the death of the Abbot of Rievaulx, he held the vill of Mewhaker (Muker) and rendered by the year

66s8d rent, he having received the Manor of Muker by a gift from the wife of Gilbert de Gaunt before her death.

In 1312 Robert, the uncle of Gilbert de Gaunt II, made to the Prior and Canons of Bridlington a gift and grant of the whole herbage of Swaledale: "in length towards the West from Herchia (Harkerside) as far as the futher torrent which is called Hawardesdalebek, and in breadth from the river Swale upwards towards the South, as far as his land extended, saving the wild beasts and the trees, and giving the said prior and canons a license to make hay in the pasture, and cut wood for houses, and folds of two vaccaries, as many as they shall need". (This gift comprised the whole Manor of Grinton.)

In 1476 AD, Edward 4th granted to Richard Duke of Gloucester, Henry, Earl of Northumberland and others, a charter for the working mines in Northumberland, Cumberland and Durham, and the copper mine at Richmond in Yorkshire, "from Lady day next for fifteen years paying to the King the eighth part neat". This grant was surrendered in three years, and the mines granted to two Germans, William Goderswick and Doderick Vaverswick.

However, the prior of Bridlington and the monks of Rievaulx Abbey were the Lords of the Manors of Grinton and Muker parishes for over two hundred years, until, at the dissolution of the monasteries during the reign of Henry VIII, the lands in Swaledale reverted to the Crown.

Henry VIII held these lands six years and afterwards leased Muker Manor to Thomas Lord Wharton in the year 1544 AD for services rendered to his king and country by defeating the Scots with great slaughter at Solway Moss. He was also granted half the Manor of Healaugh in Swaledale by Philip and Mary in 1556 and later bought the other half of the manor from Sir Thomas Vachall.

Grinton Manor remained in the hands of the Crown and was sold by Queen Elizabeth in 1599 to Richard Wiseman, goldsmith, and Francis Fitch of London, on payment of the sum of £1463-1-2d along with an annual ground rent of 40/-. In this agreement the Queen reserved the mining rights, along with the Grinton rectory and advowson. She also took a great interest in the development of the mines in England and made many grants of mining ground during her reign. In the year 1565 she caused to be founded two joint stock companies the 'Mines Royal' and the 'Society for the Mineral and Battery Works' with 'power of controlling all operations connected with the finding of ores of all kinds, of extracting the metals from them and of fashioning them for merchandising'. (Williams.)

During the reign of Queen Elizabeth many German miners were introduced into England from the Hartz Mountains, to develop the lead mining fields, on account of their superior technical knowledge of mining and smelting practice. Their knowledge of mining technique at that date – 1556 – is evidenced in Agricola's 'De Re Metallica'. It was far ahead of mining practice in Swaledale up to the 18th century, when we find some

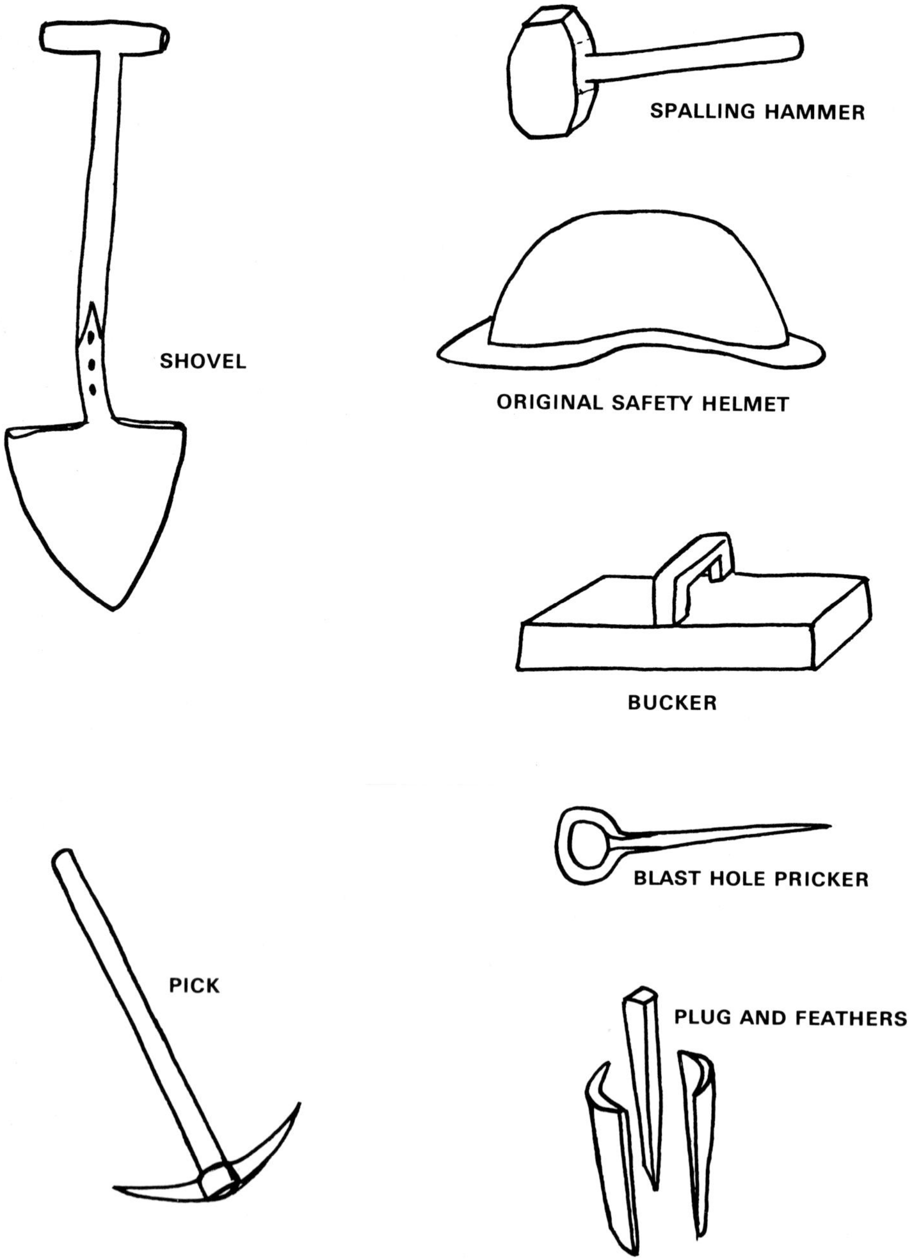

OLD MINING EQUIPMENT (B.L.)

progress had been made – probably due to the introduction of gunpowder.

The Swaledale mines continued to expand, even though they were worked by old fashioned methods. That the district had become an important mining centre is demonstrated by the records of a trial in the Court of Chancery in the year 1618–19 AD, between Philip Lord Wharton and his tenants in the Muker parish. Reference is made to the lead mines and, in the decree issued by the court, many reservations were made in favour of the lord of the manor, such as the rights to turn watercourses for mining purposes, the rights to all timber on the commons and sole right to all the mines found anywhere in the manor. These with a view to the future development of the lead mining industry, which at that early date had begun to expand rapidly.

The benevolent Philip Lord Wharton built a small dissenters' chapel (outside the 5 mile limit) for the use of dissenters and his miners in the adjacent lead mines. This Chapel near Low Row was named Smarber Chapel and registered at Thirsk Oct 8th 1691.

Contemporary events in Derbyshire paralleled the development of the Swaledale mines when, in 1692 AD, the 'Governor and Company for Smelting Lead ores with Pit or Sea Coal' was formed by quakers. The quaker London Lead Company soon built up a strong base in the Alston area. Later, they also operated mines in Swaledale when small private companies were formed to lease mining ground from the lord of the manor on a royalty basis.

Another factor in the expansion of the mines was the introduction of gunpowder for blasting operations.

Previous to the manors of Muker and Healaugh being leased to Lord Wharton, the lead mining in the dale had been carried on, probably, by the Priors of Bridlington and the Abbots of Rievaulx, chiefly for private use. Hence there was little competition or effort made by them to develop the lead trade during these times. At many of the old monasteries and baronial castles, smelting hearths have been found, where lead was smelted for use in ecclesiastical buildings and other purposes in which lead was required. The Cistercians of Rievaulx were interested in mining in many parts of Yorkshire and we cannot but infer they would be mining for lead in Swaledale during their ownership.

Prior to the 18th century, lead mining was carried on as a secondary occupation to agriculture by the inhabitants of the dale. Local economic conditions no doubt greatly facilitated the rapid development of the mining area in Swaledale after the formation of the small mining companies in the early 18th century. The companies had available a highly skilled body of miners with the experience of generations of their forebears, which fortunate circumstances made the development of the mines a rapid and easy task. Today, if any mining operations were contemplated, the miners would have to be imported. Quite a contrast to the conditions which prevailed two hundred years ago.

18th Century Developments

Until German miners introduced the technique of draining mines by drainage level or 'soughs' it was impossible to work below the level of the natural water table. Some of the oldest mines were open cast work along the outcrop of a vein. Others were 'bell pits'. Many bell pits are still to be seen on the fells around Swaledale. They look like shallow saucer shaped depressions and there may be long columns of them following the course of a vein. Miners dug a vertical shaft on the vein until they were thwarted from further downward progress by the waterlogging of their workings. Then they proceeded to dig horizontally, following the vein as far as they dared until there was imminent danger of a collapse.

If the sides of the workings were precarious, a system of timbering was used. The pieces of wood used for this purpose along the sides of the shaft were called 'sliders', those at the end 'forks'. If the earth around the shaft sides was very loose, the miners used smaller timber which they thrust behind the sliders. These they called 'stoprods'.

With earlier and more primitive methods, mines had frequently been abandoned owing to water difficulties, but with the advent of the steam engine many of them were restarted.

In the 15th and 16th centuries, and earlier, lead ore was sought by individuals or small groups of men under temporary arrangements made by themselves for some particular undertaking or trial – with the consent of the owner of the mineral rights who received a royalty varying from 1/4 to 1/8 of the produce of the mine.

A piece of ground believed to be promising would be selected by the miners, and a permit obtained from the Lord of the Manor or his agent. The portion taken over for exploitation was a given number of meers in the direction of the vein. The meer was equivalent to about 30 yards. The term regularly occurs in old bargains or leases. Another measure covered the distance the miners were permitted to work on each side of the vein. This area was known as the 'quarter cord' and varied, as agreed upon, from 7½ yards upwards. The miners' right to work did not extend beyond the limit fixed, although the length of the quarter cord was often 'stretched' to encourage exploration in difficult ground.

A second factor in the development of 18th century mining was the formation of Companies of Adventurers, formed for working mines for lead.

An interesting light is thrown on these old mining days by a document in which Lord Pomfret – afterwards the Earl of Pomfret – set out his views as to how the business of mining should be conducted. If not flattering to the Yorkshire character the document contains some shrewd observations which illustrate the risks and difficulties encountered by the 18th century non-resident Mines Adventurer.

Lord Pomfret was the plaintiff in the protracted Pomfret versus Smith case regarding ownership of mining rights on Beldi Hill, above Crackpott

Hall. Pomfret lost the case but re-opened proceedings time and time again until he was financially ruined. His tenacity emphasises that far more than mere principle was involved; ownership of the mineral rights was a very sound financial acquisition.

"The only way," wrote his lordship in 1773, "to have a just account and to make a full profit of the estates of the mines in Swaledale is not to employ anyone as steward who is a Yorkshire man . . . ." He went on to criticise the system of letting ground for mining and suggested several ways by which a mineral owner could avoid being cheated:

"The custom that has been practised to work the Mines by bing Tail. (Bing is a measure which ought to produce a 3rd of a fodder) (that is to say by so many bings of rough ore before it is smelted) opening a door to the principal Agent and under Agents, to cheat, without a Possibility of Detection; because if let to any of their friends and relations, they will pay for the ore when but half drest, or mixed with dirt as if it was pure ore, whilst they will compell others to whom they owe no good will, to sift out all the dross, so that one bing of the latter shall be worth nearly two of the formers getting. Besides they have the Power, to serve some shafts better with wood and material for mining than others; which causes great heart

Jack rollers were used to wind ore at small mines. (Carole Pugh)

burning in the fields, and gives the agents an absolute power of enriching themselves and their friends, at the loss of the proprietors, and the ruin of the credit of the mines.

"I therefore would recommend it to let all the mines at a certain fixed duty to adventurers."

This idea, and recommendations of limitations on letting of mining ground, would not have been productive in the advancement of Swaledale mining because veins and working conditions were of variable quality. Only the most productive grounds would have been let; the poorer areas remaining untried and undeveloped. Despite Lord Pomfret's cynicism, exploration and development of new mines continued apace. Mining by means of shaft and adit levels at foot was prevalent all over the dale.

The 18th century saw the commencement of many mines which were to become the famous mines of the next century – many of them household names to the present day. We find mines recorded at Higher and Lower Birkdale, Keldside, Beldi Hill, Kisdon, Glover Gill, Swinnergill, Spout Gill, Beezy, Satron Moor, Summer Lodge, Whitaside, Harkerside, Gunnerside Gill, Blakethwaite, Merryfield, Old Gang, and Hurst; in fact, on the face of every moor shafts were sunk into the upper reaches of the veins, where the miners of an earlier day had worked under more difficult conditions.

It was at this period when the method of surface working known as 'hushing' was used to a great extent. Evidence remains on many a broken hillside.

Hushing is a very old but effective method of procuring lead ore. It was probably used in pre Roman days and may have come to the islands with the Celts from the Continent. Pliny describes the process in his 'National History'. As Swaledale is a hilly area it lends itself to this method of working.

In the first place a considerable declivity is necessary. Secondly, a good supply of water must be obtainable as a source to supply a dam. The larger the capacity of the dam the better it is for the work which the water has to perform.

Many of these old dams used for hushing can be found on the moors of the district. Often they obtained their supplies of water from small streams, rivulets or springs draining the watershed above the dam. Complicated systems of leats were constructed to channel more water into the dams.

Having found a suitable vein, downhill of their dam, the miners dug out a V shaped channel or gutter from the dam to the vein. The water was then allowed to escape down the hush gutter and all the loose surface material was carried away by its force, exposing the vein. Whilst more water was collected in the dam, the miners were busy with picks and crowbars loosening the exposed vein. Towards the bottom of the hush a grating was placed over a declivity. Small pieces of ore would fall through the grating and be collected in the hollow beneath. Again the water was released to

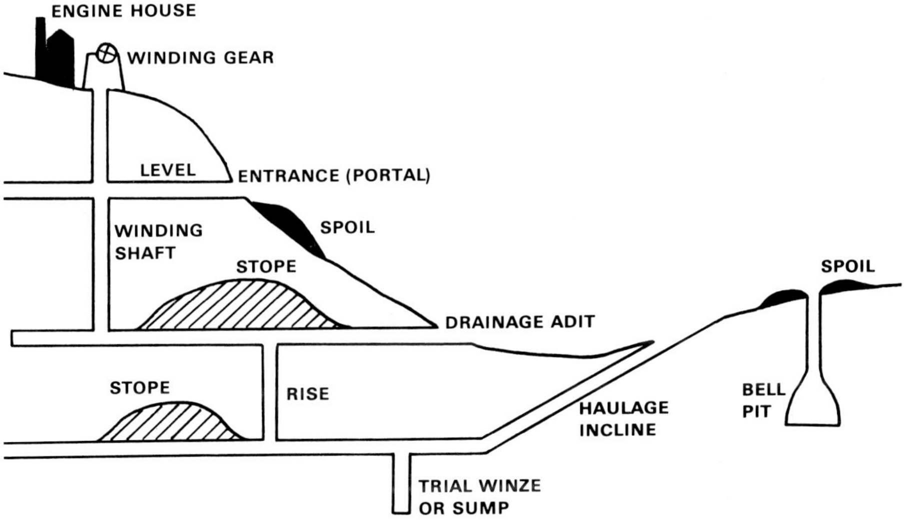

DIAGRAMMATIC EXPLANATION OF MINING TERMS (B.L.)

wreak its havoc. Large pieces of ore could be picked from the bed of the hush and small pieces from behind the grating. The more lightweight stones and gangue minerals were washed down to the Swale.

The bed of the River Swale has, in many places, been filled up by thousands of tons of debris brought into it down the old hush gutters. For several miles below the 'Old Field Hush' near Beldi Hill the bed of the Swale has been filled with stones which have been brought down the hush gutter.

The 'Old Field Hush' near Crackpot Hall was working in the 18th century and was old then. The last time it was worked was about the year 1846 when James Kearton of Muker, along with twenty men, made a bargain with the Beldi Hill Co. to work the hush again. Here several veins cross each other, with the inevitable result, that the ground is much broken up and favourable for hushing.

Two dams were made, one to the east of the hush and another towards the north west, and work commenced. The place proved so productive that the twenty two men worked there for sixteen years and got thousands of tons of lead ore. A tramway was laid from the hush to the Beldi Hill dressings and the ore was dressed and smelted there.

The writer's father was one of the men working there.

This hush would probably be the last one to work in Swaledale, the river authorities not viewing these undertakings with favour.

All the time the Old Field Hush was working two men were on duty at night and day, in all weathers, attending to the dams on Hall Moor, where two huts were built for shelter.

The distances from the two dams not being equal, this necessitated one dam being opened before the other. So the men had to signal to each other. One of them loosed his dam a considerable time after the other, so that the two streams met together at the head of the hush, giving it maximum power to break up the debris loosened by the men.

The strata around Beldi Hill were worked at much greater depths than could be reached by hushing. One remarkable piece of ore was found in Landy Level. It was a solid block of ore occupying several square yards and weighing many tons. Before stoping it the miners had to work a passage around it. On the whole, Landy Level was not very productive and was abandoned in 1882. Towards closure there were only four men employed at the mine. Two of them – Mr S. Raw of Muker and James Allinson of Brierfield – had an alarming experience.

After firing a shot during blasting operations they heard, from their temporary retreat, the ominous rush of a great volume of water.

Realising their danger they rushed along the narrow drift and down the

Old Field Hush. (Carole Pugh)

rise. On reaching the bottom the older man flung his younger companion into an empty truck and made for the entrance. This was barely reached before the water overtook them. It was later found that the rise down which they had escaped had been completely destroyed by the rush of water which blasting operations had released from flooded old workings.

19th Century

Progressing onwards into the 19th century, and over the moors to Brandy Bottle Incline at the Old Gang Mines, a disaster story occurred with a much more tragic ending

At the beginning of the 19th century a horse driven gin was used to wind ore to the surface. An endless rope, attached to the winding apparatus, was used to draw wagons up the incline. A young woman named Betty Lockey operated the winding gear. Her nephew was employed at the mine as assistant to his father. Their work involved stone-arching the mine – a dangerous occupation as arching was only required in areas where the mine was unsafe. One Good Friday – a public holiday – the mine was deserted except for the father and son who had decided to continue working. (Arching was piecework.)

After a hard day's work the men were getting ready to leave their task and were striking out the centres (supports) from their newly completed work. There was a sudden collapse of the archway and the young man was buried under tons of rock debris.

The horror stricken father worked frantically to free his trapped son who was in considerable pain and crying piteously. His frenzied efforts

At large mines horse gins were used to power winding gear. (Carole Pugh)

were all to no avail as his son was pinned to the ground by a large boulder.

Almost demented, the father left his son and started for Gunnerside to get help. There he was met by his wife who, on the premonition of coming ill, had started from home to meet her husband and son. Immediately, she ran off towards the mine, easily outstripping the band of rescuers who were also hurrying to the scene of the disaster. She had never been to the mine before but it is recorded that she rushed headlong down the dark passages without light, passing safely the ends of several mine roads and two deep sumps before reaching her son. When the rescue party arrived they found her vainly tearing at the rock to free her son who had been dead for some time.

As the 19th century progressed, safety became of greater importance. A mines inspectorate was formed and safety regulations were introduced. Better and more powerful equipment was used to drain and drive levels. Workings could be extended into untapped reserves of ore.

To illustrate the problems which were involved in winning ore from the lead veins of Swaledale in the 19th century it is interesting to study the progress made in the driving of Sir Francis Level – the last large scale mining enterprise in Swaledale.

This last level to be driven in Gunnerside Gill was begun in June 1864. It was the joint enterprise of the Blakethwaite and Old Gang companies.

The two companies had a common interest and object. They had worked the Friarfold and Old Rake veins for many years. Both had reached the lowest depths possible in the Sir George and Priscilla mines until these were waterlogged. To cut the veins at a lower level, and unwater the workings above, a joint venture was proposed.

The ground was surveyed and it was found that the proposed adit would be 43 fathoms lower than the Priscilla Level and 35 fathoms below the Sir George Level. If driven forward to the Blakethwaite vein, the Blakethwaite workings would be intersected 33 fathoms below the Blakethwaite engine sump which was 40 fathoms deep.

Thus the whole of the Friarfold vein complex would be unwatered and made workable to far greater depths.

The driving of the level through the grit beds proved an expensive and arduous task. The first 250 fathoms cost 10 guineas per fathom. Dissatisfied with the slow progress, Sir George Denys, the mineral owner, proposed to install an air compressor and boring machinery and undertook to bear this expense personally. He contracted to drive the level forward for 500 fathoms at the rate of £8-10-0d per fathom (£4,250). The Old Gang Co. were to pay 4/5 of this and the Blakethwaite Co. 1/5. (Two years afterwards, the Blakethwaite Co. was dissolved and a new company formed – the A.D. Co. – with a share capital of £20,000.)

The compressor and boring machinery were installed at a cost of £650. The borers worked at 70lb pressure per square inch and averaged four inches per minute when boring a hole for blasting purposes.

In driving the level, several veins were intersected. After 400 fathoms' driving Barbara Vein was met with, and at 630 fathoms Water Sykes Vein was reached. At 748 fathoms the Friarfold and Old Rake veins were intersected. At this point it was found that they had united, forming one vein.

This happy event was accomplished on March 12, 1877, amidst great rejoicing.

Sir George Denys writes in his notebook, "Monday, March 12, 1877. Friarfold Vein was cut in Sir Francis. Great jubilation thereon, 13 years labour finished triumphantly without loss, but also without profit. The profit will be in the future, for the men who will find plenty of employment for generations. For the Lessees who will get a return for their Capital, and for the lessors who will get the Royalty. It is a fine strong vein, with plenty of life in it. The cost of driving the level up to its point of intersection with the Fryerfold Vein was a little over £6000, and cost over £600 to drive in the explosives alone."

After cutting the vein, the Old Gang Co. commenced driving off to the East and after driving 5 fathoms commenced rising in the vein to prove the break.

The A.D. Co., which was formed in 1870 from the Old Blakethwaite Co., commenced driving west in the Vein and had good ore for a short distance, but this gradually decreased until the vein was full of nothing but grit and plate for a distance of 27 fathoms, when the ore set in again. By the time the A.D. boundary was reached it became very good both in the level and the roof.

By August 3rd 1878 the A.D. Co. had raised 1,200 bings of ore and the prospects of the mine were rosy. Success seemed certain.

The ore in the level sole was followed downwards and it was decided to sink a shaft down to the 5th Limestone, to be operated by a powerful hydraulic engine which was installed in February, 1881, at a cost of £4,500, and was supplied with water from a dam on the moor above.

To accomplish this object a shaft was sunk from the surface a distance of about 43 fathoms, and down this shaft huge cast iron pipes conveyed the water from the Sun Hush Dam on the moor above, down to the engine which developed 50 horse power. The engine both pumped the water from the sump and worked the cages which raised the ore and miners.

The shaft to the surface, also the engine sump, was supported by very strong timbers, 12" square pitch/pine sliders and forks being used to support the sides. The Old Gang Co. also had an hydraulic engine and sump on their side, but not so powerful as the one installed by the A.D. Co. Theirs was found unequal to the work it had to perform.

The A.D. engine sump reached the vein in the 5th limestone where it was found to be 8 feet wide and contained good ore. A rib on the south cheek of the vein was 3" to 4" wide and of solid ore. From the sump a productive adit level – Tiplady's Drift – was driven.

The main level in the vein was continued to the Great Lowanthwaite break, cutting Blind Gill and Water Sykes veins. Then it was extended under Priscilla Level to make available the reported reserves of ore which had, previously, been unobtainable because of drainage problems. For ventilation and drainage purposes, two rises were excavated upwards into Priscilla Level. They accomplished the object of ventilating the mine but little ore was found. No ore was obtained from Water Sykes vein in the lower beds of Sir Francis level.

On completion of the ore dressing plant in September 1879 a festival was held at Sir Francis level to commemorate the event. All the men employed at the mines, and their wives and families, were invited. A band provided music and many speeches and songs added to the enjoyment of the entertainment. The health of the directors and future success of the mine was toasted in 30 gallons of beer. Sir George Denys records that all the miners went home very happy.

Sir Francis Level gained ore worth £32,000 for the A.D. Co.

To dress such a large amount of ore a large water wheel (28′10″ in diameter and 4′8″ in breadth) was used to power the crushing and washing machinery. Installation of machinery cost £1113-18-4d.

Ore from Old Gang workings was brought out at Sir Francis Level, conveyed to Bunting Level and taken back underground. From Bunting Level it was dropped down a hopper into Hard Level, then taken out to the Old Gang dressing floor in Hard Level Gill. When processed, it was ready for smelting at the nearby Old Gang smelt mill.

In 1882, due to the low price of lead (£9 per ton) work at the mine was almost entirely suspended; only a few men continued to work until 1900.

The engine sump filled with water, and a mining venture of great possibilities came to an end as the A.D. Co. failed to raise the necessary money to carry on.

During the whole of their operations accidents were, happily, rare but, unfortunately, fatalities were not unknown.

During the working of Sir Francis, three men were killed – Joseph Brunskill of Muker, Christopher Bell and James Bell. James Bell, 58 years old, was working in Sir Francis, and had retired during the firing of a shot into a neighbouring working. As the shot detonated, the sides of the workings collapsed, letting down the head tree and cover wood above and releasing a cascade of deads. Bell was killed instantly.

Another man, Anthony Cottingham, was severely injured by a dynamite explosion during the driving of Sir Francis level. The explosive was frozen so he attempted to thaw it out in hot water, whereupon it exploded. Fortunately, the injured man made a good recovery.

In 1904, during the operation of rising from Sir Francis into Priscilla, after rising 12 fathoms in the 10 fathom grit an explosion of firedamp occurred when two miners, S. & T. Rutter, were working. Fortunately they were not much burnt. This explosion was unprecedented in the history of mining in Swaledale and its occurrence caused much alarm.

In 1878 James Tiplady was injured in the engine house by being caught in the spur wheels and had four toes cut off.

Sir Francis Mine, air receiver tank. (B.L.)

Old Gang Smelt Mill. (B.L.)

Ore Dressing

Bouse – the mixture of ore, stone and pieces of other minerals – had to be sorted and cleaned before smelting. A good supply of water was of prime importance both for cleaning the ore and, via a waterwheel, as a source of power for grinding and crushing. Dams were constructed all over the moor and elaborate systems of leats conveyed water to the dressing floors which were usually situated at the mouth of a haulage level.

The dressing process relies on the fact that the specific gravities of the individual constituents of the bouse were all different. Lead ore (galena) had the highest specific gravity.

One cubic foot of galena or lead ore weighs from 7300 to 78000 ounces, according to purity. It varies a little in many mines. One bing of galena weighs roughly 14,336 ounces, and from this the mineral contents of a given length of vein with a given rib of galena can be calculated; e.g.

Inches wide of Ore	Feet high	Feet long	Cu. ft.	Bings	Cwt	qr	lb	oz
1	6	6	3	1	3	2	24	8
2	6	6	6	2	7	1	21	0

If we take a riddle or sieve and put into it a quantity of small bouse and thrust the riddle and its contents briskly downwards into a tub of water, then repeat the operation several times, on examination of the contents of the riddle it will be found that the lightest material has been thrust to the surface and the heavier lead ore deposited at the bottom. All the various constituents of the bouse will be stratified into layers according to their specific gravity, making it possible to scrape off the lightest stones from the top.

The next layer beneath the stones consists of pieces of stone with ore attached, or stone with ore disseminated through the mass. This layer is removed and undergoes further treatment. These are called chats and are to bucker or, where motive power is employed, they are ground finely between the rollers of the grinding machine.

At the bottom of the riddle we shall find pure lead ore in small pieces. At the bottom of the tub we should find very fine lead which had escaped through the meshes of the riddle. This is called 'smuddum'. It would be mixed with a small amount of sand. The whole process is known as sotching or hotching.

In the sotching process a large square timber tub is used, into which a square sieve or riddle is supported from a long lever or arm called the stang. When the stang is elevated the sieve is plunged below the water level and a series of jerks given to it by the operator. The motion separates the ore from the stone material exactly as the hand sieve operated in the description given above. The material is removed from the sieve by a wooden and iron tool called the limp.

Before the introduction of the sotching tub hand sieves were used. The first washing the bouse undergoes is called grating, which consists of allowing a strong current of water to flow over a grate upon which a quantity of bouse to be washed has been placed. It is then raked backwards and forwards so as to make all the small ore and stones pass through the grate down a launder to the trunking box. This is removed and is ready for the sotching tub process.

Any ore that is too large to pass through the grate is hand picked from the grate and ready for the bingstead for smelting.

After the introduction of water wheels, to power grinding mills, the process of grating was unnecessary. The crushed material was ready to go direct to the sotching process.

During the dressing process, a considerable quantity of very fine ore escapes in the water. It is collected in large settling pits called slime or sludge pits. Ore is removed from the sludge by the process of 'buddling'.

The simplest form of buddle consisted of a wide wooden launder or trough, about 1 yard wide and two to three yards long, slightly inclined, and through which a constant evenly distributed current of water flowed. The slime was shovelled slowly into the buddle by a workman, and was carried and intermixed by the current of water. The ore, being heavy, immediately settled and was kept at the top of the buddle by a boy who sat on a board across the buddle. Using a wooden 'cowlrake' he kept the ore at the top end of the buddle, allowing the fine mud and sand to escape in suspension in the water. This apparatus was called a 'trunk buddle'.

Water wheels powered ore dressing machinery. This wheel at Bunton Level in Gunnerside Gill was removed many years ago. (Carole Pugh)

In the days of hand dressing, the bouse obtained by each partnership of miners was dressed by contract at a certain price per bing. If rich ore was mined, the dressing price might be as low as two to three shillings per bing. Low grade bouse required more attention and could cost from five to eight shillings per bing. The dressing cost was borne by the miners who had to deliver dressed ore, ready for smelting, to the masters.

Much female and child labour was employed in ore dressing. It was a difficult, cold job. The winter days, when water courses were frozen over and no water was available for dressing, must have provided a welcome respite from the hardships of the task. However, a long freeze could bring ore dressing to a standstill for many weeks and was the cause of a great deal of temporary poverty in the dale.

Smelting

Lead ore ideally contains about 87% of lead and 13% sulphur. The smelting process was necessary to change brittle galena into malleable lead by driving off its sulphur content.

In some parts of the country a valuable by-product of the smelting process was silver. This was extracted by the additional process of cupellation. However, the proportion of silver in Swaledale ore rarely exceeded 3 ounces per ton and was considered to be uneconomical to

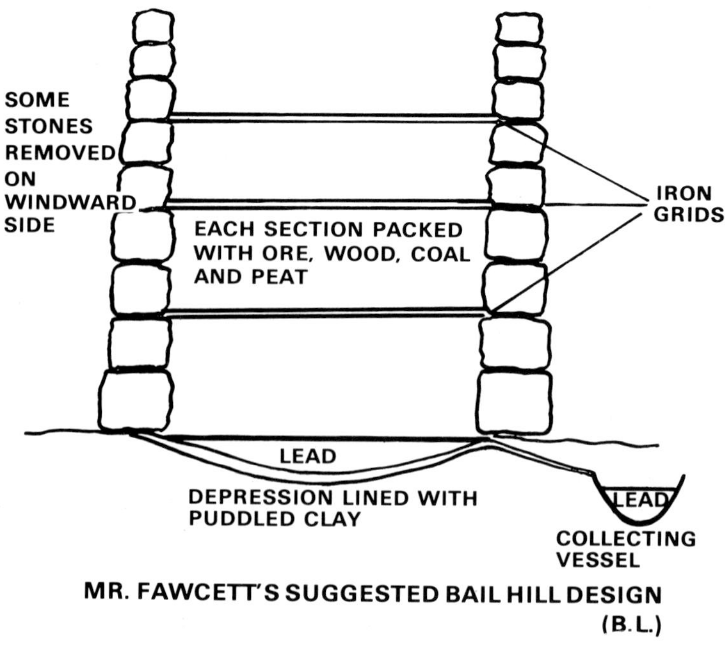

MR. FAWCETT'S SUGGESTED BAIL HILL DESIGN
(B.L.)

extract. This small percentage of silver made Swaledale lead a little harder and more durable than imported lead.

Before the introduction of ore hearth smelting a primitive method of smelting was used. A hill was selected – generally one well exposed to the strong westerly and south-westerly winds – and as near as possible to the site of the mine. A circular stone wall, about 2 feet high, was erected. One side was not completed, for the better admission of air to the fire which burnt inside and which was supplied with ore plus fuel from the neighbouring moors and woods. The name baal or bail hill was given to these rude smelting places.

A basin shaped depression was constructed under the fire. From this the lead ran down a channel which led into a receptacle which was periodically emptied into an oblong iron mould to produce finished pigs of lead.

This is the generally accepted idea of the methods employed in the baal hill smelting but the writer has heard old men describe the process differently:

The circular wall, with openings for air, was made as a support for a number of iron rails which formed the base of the fire. On this base was placed wood and peat – then a layer of ore was placed on the peat. This operation was repeated until there were several layers of ore separated by fuel. A basin shaped depression was made under the fire, from which a channel led to a receptacle, under which was kept a fire to keep the lead liquid till sufficient was stored to make a pig.

On a favourable day, with strong, constant winds, much more ore could be smelted by this process than by the primitive bail hill method.

The first introduction of the blast hearth method of smelting seems to have been at Marske. A lead smelting mill is recorded there in 1590. From that date there are numerous records.

The ore hearths where the lead was smelted were not unlike an ordinary blacksmith's hearth. The ore hearth fire was rectangular in form and about 24 inches long, 12 inches broad and 22 inches deep. The side walls of the fire box consisted of cast iron blocks, one of the blocks having at its base a hole through which protruded the bellows nozzle. At the bottom of the fire box was the pan or well which was a one piece casting.

The internal part of the iron box was filled with peats, which, when lighted, and aided by the blast from the bellows, soon developed a high temperature which was increased by an occasional few coals. Coals were used sparingly.

When the temperature was sufficiently high, ore was put on the fire. The intense heat gradually dissociated the sulphur from the galena, the liquid lead trickling through the fire into the pan below. When this was full, lead overflowed down a channel into a small heated receptacle from which lead was ladled into moulds.

During smelting a quantity of lead was vaporized and escaped into the flues along with the smoke. The amount of lead vaporized was 3 to 5 grains of lead per cubic foot of smoke. To prevent waste, and to recover this lead, the chimneys, or flues, from the smelting mills were made a great length – often half a mile. This length allowed the smoke plenty of time to cool and deposit its load of lead and soot.

Chimneys and flues were cleaned at regular intervals by diverting a stream into the highest portion of the chimney. Men were employed with cowl rakes to clean soot from the sides of the flues and mix it with water flowing down the chimney. The work was often hazardous, particularly when compounds of arsenic were present in the sulphurous fumes.

The mixture emptied into a settling house, built at the base of the chimney, and was allowed to dry until it had the consistency of clay. Then it was dug out and removed to the roasting furnace where the carbon was burnt off. After the residue had been broken up into small pieces it was smelted at the ordinary hearths.

The flues were generally about 4 to 5 feet in height and 3 feet wide, several hundreds of yards long, and built on the slopes of a hill, ending in an upright chimney.

Several sad accidents are recorded, where men have lost their lives by loosing their hold on the sides and being carried down by the water and heavy soot to be smothered in the pit below.

The lead produced at the ore hearths was the purest and best. However, the process was wasteful. A scum, or slag, or lighter material floated to the surface and was discarded. When it was realised that this process was wasteful, many of the larger mills introduced an extra hearth to smelt the slag. Slag hearths operated at a higher temperature in order to drive off oxygen from the oxides of lead contained in the slag. The waste material from slag hearths is usually black and glassy in texture, whereas that from ore hearths has a dull grey appearance.

The lead produced from a slag hearth was not as pure as that from the ore hearth and pigs were stamped with the word 'slagg'. They were of lower commercial value.

At the various mines the smelting process found employment for a large number of men and boys. Most of the work was done by contract at a given price per ton of lead; the average price being 6/- to 7/- per ton.

The Old Gang smelting hearths in 1859 were producing 800 pigs of lead per week and 403 cwts of grey slag for further smelting at the slag hearths.

The smelters marked all the pigs with a capital letter. Starting at the letter A they smelted a 'mark' – 400 pieces – before changing to letter B and so on through the alphabet.

This was in addition to the trade mark initials of the mine or mining co. where the lead was produced.

This marking was of great service to the trade as, when marketed, consignments were known by the letters stamped on them. Their number being stated, loss or theft could be easily detected and traced during transit.

Grinton Smelt Mill. (Carole Pugh)

Marketing and Shipping of Lead

Little is known of the early lead trade except that there are references to lead being sold at Richmond and Barnard Castle.

The earliest definite shipping of Swaledale lead is recorded in an old book in the Guildhall at York, which contains the sales, 'strekyng' (marking) and weighing of lead at the Old Crane, Skeldergate during the year 1560–1561 A.D.

Listed are the names of many Swaledale and Wensleydale mine owners, viz. Pigs, marked I F, John Fawcett, T. Watson 24th March 10 cwt lead, Sir Christopher Metcalfe, Mr Pacocks, Master Sayer, George Pette, Thos Hutchinson and Raff Hall are all dale names and each had their respective lead marks.

At the end of the book is a summary of

	£	s	d
The tenant of the crane claimed for fees	6	0	0
For a bucket and besomes			8
Sum for 'hendyng' and weighing	11	11	10
Sum for 'Strekynge' 500 peces at 3/4 per 100		16	8
For 'Wyndyg' and 'Strykeyrge'	2	5	8
	£20	14	10

Hendyng (handling)

After the claims of the owner of the crane a balance was left of £14-14-2d to city funds.

This lead was possibly carted by road to York, or to the nearest point on the river, after which it may have been conveyed by water to the crane on the Ouse bank.

No addresses of buyers or factors of York are noted in the account book.

During the whole of the 18th century and part of the 19th the Swaledale and Arkengarthdale lead was conveyed by horses and carts to the lead yard at Richmond, the carts returning home loaded with mine timber etc.

After the railway was constructed to Richmond, all the lead was carted by horses to Richmond station. The writer has heard old men relate that they had seen the station goods yard packed with heaps of pig lead awaiting a rise of price in the lead market. When that happy event materialized the whole of the lead was sold and despatched in a few days.

From Richmond it was carted to the lead yard at Darlington and subsequently transferred to Yarm or Stockton for shipment to either London, Newcastle upon Tyne or the Continent.

Our present day knowledge of the lead trade of Stockton would have been very meagre if the letters and books of the shipper and lead agent of Stockton, Mr Matthew Wadeson, had not been preserved. He was the agent for the years 1781 to 1810.

Mr Wadeson was agent for the C B Mines in Arkengarthdale owned by Mr Hoar and partners. In a letter to that gentleman, June 20th 1795, he writes: "Dear Mr Hoar, I am returned from the Arkendale Mines, where we had a very heavy day indeed, our quota £1957-1-4, but tis some satisfaction to find 22 Marks – 8800 pieces of lead – has been raised the last half year. If you are disposed to sell I think 15 guineas or £16 may be obtained for a mark or two, from the Lead Co. at Newcastle; they have an offer of one Mark from Col. Sleigh (also a partner).

In 1796 he writes: "A good deal of lead sent to Hull intended for this market." (The Hull fodder, 21 cwt, was less in weight than the Stockton fodder of 22 cwts.) All lead at that date was sold by the fodder and it probably paid some owners better to ship to Hull. In one of his letters he refers to the war with France which was declared on Feb 3, 1793.

The war affected the Stockton lead trade, as the ships had to convoy to London and the Continent. Occasionally a French privateer made them seek shelter at Scarborough or some other port. The war had such an effect on the lead trade that prices got as low as £15 per fodder at Stockton. Lead of inferior quality and slag lead brought much lower prices.

In one of Mr Wadeson's letters to Col. Sleigh, 1798, regarding the price of lead, he says: "I cannot hear that any are disposed to follow Doubleday & Easterby of Newcastle in their price for lead. Yet the holders of best sorts are standing at £21, that they do so I'm persuaded as much from the small stocks in market, as from prospect of peace."

The charges for shipping recorded by Mr Wadeson were: Stockton to London – 12/6 per ton, at owner's risk. This price at times fluctuated several shillings.

As agent for several lead firms Mr Wadeson had 1% commission on all lead he bought. The bulk of his purchases went to Messrs. Walkers, Maltby & Co., London.

He also shipped all the A D lead for Peter Denys to Mr Jas Hague, London.

This noted mark of lead 'A D' had a great reputation on the continent and consignments went to Sweden, Holland, Hamburg, St Petersburg and many other continental ports. (N.B. The 'A D' mark was again used by a later company, previously referred to – the re-formed Blakethwaite Co. of Sir Francis mine.)

Mr Wadeson also recorded the scarcity of lead in the markets due to the hard winters when the roads from the mines to Stockton were impassable with snow, and navigation impossible in the river due to ice. Also the difficulty experienced at times due to torrential floods in the river, which made navigation impossible.

The Stockton vessels which shipped most of the lead, 1791–1810, were:

The Hawk	Chris Pearson, Master
The Satisfaction	Robert Norman, Master

The Union	Chris Burnicle, Master
The Expedition	Robt. Medd, Master
The Friends Adventure	Robt. Burnicle, Master
The Eagle	Robt. Davison, Master
The Neptune	Henry Terry, Master
The Stockton	Jas Graham, Master
The Loyalty	Wm Watern, Master
The Darlington	Robt. Barrett, Master
The Stockton Packet	M. D. Grear, Master
The Friendship	Wm Hansill, Master
The Griffin	Robt Davison, Master
The Isabella	I. Bowron, Master
The Laurel (sloop)	Richd. Hudson, Master
The Rosetta	I. Allison, Master
The Despatch	Wm Claxton, Master

It was customary for these vessels to carry a portion of their lead freight as ballast (at low rates) at certain times of the year. When the corn and pork trade commenced lead had to be charged at the usual rates.

Two bills of lading were issued for each cargo; one to the recipient of the lead and the other to the ship's master. An example is given below:

Character, Marks, and Weights, of 1095 Pieces Lead.
Shipped for P. Denys, Esq., to James Hague, London, by Mattw. Wadeson

1792									
Sep 30	In the Griffin, Robt Davison								
AD 99	Pieces Lead Letter W	137	2	3					
AD 100	Pieces Lead Letter T	138	3	4					
AD 299	Pieces Lead Letter U	416	1	3					
AD 300	Pieces Lead Letter Z	412	1	11					
AD 100	Pieces Lead Letter A	156	1	27					
AD 100	Pieces Lead Letter B	158	1	27					
AD 97	Pieces Lead Letter N	134	1	18		tons	cwts	qrs	lbs
1095	pieces weight cwts	1554	1	8	=	77	14	1	8

	FODDERS	CWTS.	QRS.	LBS.		
OR	70	14	1	8	@ £20 per foddr	£1413- 0- 4

Sepr. Ex on Shipg. Union, Chrisr. Burnside	£18- 7- 4
Griffin, Robt Davison	20-10- 4
	£ 38-17- 8

All the pieces of lead were stamped with the company's initial letters and also with mark letters. Thus each pig of lead was readily identifiable.

When lead was shipped to foreign ports in neutral ships (presumably to

Lead was traded at Richmond. (B.L.)

avoid the French privateers) a landing certificate had to be signed by the resident British Consul.

Landing Certificate

I the undersigned, do hereby certify and attest that Mr Immanuel Frederick Godelman, have landed at this Port Sept 29th 1804 – five hundred and forty six pieces of Lead (546) – Shipped from Stockton on the 15th Sept 1804 – By Mathew Wadeson pr ship the Vack Maria Johnna, Master Floris Perleflich – Given under my Hand & Seal of Office at Emden Cot 25 1804

Kings
Arms

Fredk Lindeman,
His Britannic Majesty's
Consul at Emden

Life in the Dale

In the early days of the mining period wages were extremely low. In the 18th century one shilling per day was the amount paid to miners per shift of eight hours. This low rate of pay obtained up to about the year 1810, when wages were paid to daymen at the rate of 1/3 to 1/6 per shift. From 1810 up to the year 1850 shiftmen earned about 10/- per week of six shifts, which shows a slight rise. From that date to 1880 the rate per shift was from 2/- to 2/6. These rates may appear very small and meagre to the reader, who must bear in mind that wages were very low throughout the country in all trades. Even so, the standard of life amongst the Swaledale miners must have been of a very low and humble order.

The small houses of this period were chiefly thatched cottages, giving scanty accommodation for large families.

In the early years of the 19th century, many of these thatched cottages were altered, an upper story was built and the roof covered with stone flag/slates. The fireplace, which in early times was the centre of the room, was built at the gable end of the house where the chimneys in some cases were built outside. These are often spoken of in old documents of the dale, as firehouses. In all the Swaledale villages most of the houses have been altered as described. An observer will notice the different building stone used for the upper story, compared with the lower. At the gable ends of the cottages may be seen the newer stones with which they have been raised to alter the pitch of the roof. In the case of stone slates the pitch is not so steep as in the thatched cottages.

On the edge of the wild moorland above Gunnerside may be seen the ruins of several of the old thatched cottages of the early miners. They were very small, and the accommodation they afforded was very limited. In the case of miners with large families, which were the order of the day, they must have left much to be desired.

One economic feature which helped the miners considerably was the modest rents of their small cottages; most of them from £1 to 30/- per year. In some instances single rooms over stables were let as low as 10/- per year. The largest and best cottages in the villages never exceeded 30/- to 40/- per year; very moderate rents compared to those prevailing in many parts of the country today.

In the early and mid 19th century the population of Swaledale was much higher than it is today as evidenced by the figures of the 1821 census compared with the 1927 census. The population in the Parishes of Swaledale in the above years was:

	1821	1927
Grinton	689	279
Marrick	621	146
Melbecks	1726	402

Brownsey Moor above Low Row. (B.L.)

Crackpot Hall. (B.L.)

Muker	1425	502
Reeth	1460	616
Ellerton	47	21

This great shrinkage of the population of Swaledale was due to the closing down of the mines and the exodus of two thirds of the population which occurred mainly between the years 1875 and 1885.

Swaledale during the mining period was the scene of many activities. The population was much larger, the majority being miners. They almost all worked on 6 or 8 hour shift systems, Sundays excepted. This system of working the mines necessitated miners changing shifts at various hours of the day and night. The moors and mining field were scarcely ever clear of men either going to work or returning. The shift system made it possible to keep employed at one mine a large number of men; in many cases several hundreds when mining was prosperous.

Most of the miners worked at the numerous shafts on the adjoining moors. Many old roads of 'jagging tracks' – which were constructed for horses and men only – can be found today on the moors, where the miners conveyed the ore they had won in sacks placed one on each side of a horse; a slow laborious means of transport compared to our present day motors. The mines, being situated in the desolate mountain ravines of the district, or on the bleak moors, were very inaccessible.

The miners had often to walk long distances – 3 to 6 miles – to and from their work. These arduous journeys at the close of a hard day's work, when perhaps they had eaten no food for several hours, had anything but a beneficial effect upon the health of the miners. Many of them died at an early age, and there is no doubt these long journeys in all sorts of weather were a contributory factor in breaking down the health of any but the most robust.

Other factors responsible for the early death of many of the miners were the conditions they worked under in the mines. Nearly all lead mines collect large quantities of water from the many veins and rock fissures. These are the drains or water channels for the surrounding rocks. Hence most of the miners had their clothes wet through at the end of each shift, due to water from the vein dripping upon them during working hours.

They often had to work in a foul atmosphere, the air being so deficient in oxygen that a candle would scarcely burn. This was due to faulty ventilation, to which might be added the chemical fumes resulting from the use of various explosives – such as gunpowder and dynamite – in enclosed workings.

The effect of these several conditions was cumulative and nearly all the miners, unless very robust, fell prey to the dreaded 'miner's consumption'. After weary years of suffering they filled an early grave.

Bargains

The arrangement between master and men, as to rates of pay for work performed was, from the miners' standpoint, a bad one. The bargain system obtained at all the mines, under which miners took contracts to win ore at a price per bing (8cwts) arranged between them and the master.

Bargains were let on a given day to partnerships which consisted of from 8 to 16 men who worked as a team. The men contracted to win a given quantity of ore at an arranged price per bing. If, at a given forehead in the mine, no ore was in view, the maximum price of 50/- to 60/- per bing was paid. If the ore in another forehead was plentiful, the price bargained for was often as low as 6/- to 10/- per bing. This system of payment led to many irregularities and loss of work and money by the miners.

Let us suppose a partnership of men had taken a bargain to win 500 bings of ore at 50/- per bing, when no ore was in view. Then after a few days working if luck came their way and they struck a rich deposit of ore, instead of working hard to win the ore and complete their bargain they idled and produced little ore so as to convince the mine manager that ore was still difficult to find. Thus the system worked against both masters and men as the mine became less productive than it should have been.

The bargain system was also ineffective in providing economic stability for the miners. Partnerships of men, if unlucky, often worked months and earned very little, if anything.

The wages of daymen – men paid by the day – was from 10/- to 12/- per week (during the first half of the 19th century). These men were spoken of as 'dead men' to distinguish them from the orewinners. N.B. Deads, or piles of unproductive rock, are often stacked in worked out parts of a mine or used as supports in unsafe areas.

Many of the dead men were engaged in driving levels by 'fathom tail' that is a certain price per fathom as agreed upon. At times when work was scarce at home the miners went to mines in the adjacent dales, taking their food, and lodging there. This was named 'carrying t' wallet'. When we consider the small wages earned and the long distances the miners had to walk to and from their work to earn a very uncertain living, we can only surmise that grim necessity compelled them to do it.

Subsist money was never advanced to the miners in Swaledale who, if they were unlucky and struck no ore, had no wages but owed the company a sum of money for candles and powder used during their trial. This was deducted from their next earnings. Such a system of payment was in striking contrast to the humane treatment meted out to the miners of the 'Governor & Co of the Quaker Co.', afterwards the 'London Lead Co.', which was incorporated Oct 4th 1692 and ended May 30th 1911.

This company had a 'Lent Money Day', instead of a pay day, when each miner was lent a definite amount of money – 10/6 per week – whether he had earned it or not. The earnings of each man were balanced up at the year end and his excess wages, above the money loaned, was paid in a lump sum. If in deficit, this was carried over into the next year.

The care of the miners under this company was beyond praise and was an example to all mining concerns throughout the country.

The nature of the miners' calling made them one and all optimists. They went to their work each day full of hope and anticipation that they would be rewarded by cutting a rich vein of ore. If they were successful they earned fairly well for a time and if failure attended their efforts they seldom complained, knowing well the uncertainties of mining. The continual gamble for a meagre living appealed to their sporting instincts and kept them toiling on, living in the future, hoping for a reward which seldom came. We can only compare them to the old pioneers of the gold fields who spent their lives under conditions of hardship and privation in their search for gold and who on their death bed would declare what a pleasure to them their work had been, and that they would enjoy living it over again; and could die without any regrets.

The economic and social conditions accruing from the uncertain wages earned by the miners left much to be desired. Most of them with large families were very poor and, we might say, below the poverty line. Practically all of them lived on the credit system, trading with the several village shops, paying for their goods at every six or eight weeks' end – when the pays were made at the mines – assuming they had earned enough money to be paid.

The 'partnership pays' – when the miners received their wages – were always held at one of the village inns. It was the custom of each partnership to allow a certain amount of money to be spent for the goodwill of the house. The money was deducted equally from each man in the partnership and if it happened that a few of them were abstainers this ensured a liberal supply of refreshments for the remainder. The final results of these paynight revelries was the setting for many a comedy, some of the miners taking on board more than their legs could safely carry to their distant homes.

A story often related refers to an old lady who kept the Kings Head Inn at Muker. The men working at one of the adjacent mines were paid their wages there. The custom in those days was to order a gallon jug of beer, then serve round to the company with a small glass and share out a drink to each person. This was named 'birling'.

Each time the men ordered a gallon of beer the old landlady made a chalk mark on the stone lintel of the fireplace. This primitive style of accountancy went on till the chalk marks numbered about one dozen, after which some member of the party would rub out a chalk mark for each one the old woman added. So, the total count was not allowed to exceed one dozen, and the pockets of the drinkers not too seriously depleted. This was considered a good joke, if not very honest.

Another incident often related refers to a partnership pay at Muker, when four miners, Paf Sol (Harker), Paff Kit Will (Harker), Cotty Kit Blick (Alderson) and Katey Will (Alderson) (nearly all the miners had nicknames), had been working at East Arngill Mine near Muker and had been extremely fortunate.

They had taken a bargain from the masters to win a given number of bings or ore. After working a few days they cut a rich portion of the vein and, working hard, got the requisite number of bings in eight weeks. They had £400 for their partnership pay. This was paid to them in current coin of the realm. After receiving it, they retired to the home of Katey Will to arrange for its equal distribution amongst the partners. Katey Will's good wife Ann, acting as cashier, commenced to divide this large sum of money. But, after several unsuccessful attempts, she suddenly arose from her seat and, grasping her shawl, exclaimed, "Chaps, wait a bit, an al away roond to t' Queens Head and borrow t' quartern mezzure an weel mezzur 't."

Food

The staple diet of most of the large families was oatmeal porridge, with skimmed milk; new milk being too expensive to use. 'Havercake' – made from oatmeal – was also much used.

Wheaten bread was not extensively used prior to the repeal of the corn laws; white flour being too expensive to buy for many of the poor, being at times as high as 6/- per stone.

Butter was a luxury to many of the poorer households and it was used sparingly.

Whole milk cheese was made by the farmers of the dale for sale but never eaten at home. For home use large quantities of skimmed milk cheese was made and consumed by both miners and farmers. Often the only occasion when either the miners or farmers tasted whole milk cheese was at Christmas or New Year, when a small cheese had been preserved for use at the festive seasons. One unfortunate characteristic of skim milk cheese was that, having had the cream extracted, it became very hard and almost uneatable. To overcome this difficulty the miners toasted their cheese in the flame of the tallow candles which they used for light in the mines. This cheese was known by the popular name of 'wangby'.

Amongst the poorer members of the community meat was seldom seen, except perhaps some of the cheaper offal portions of the carcase, such as the heads and plucks. Pluck consisted of lungs, heart and liver. These were placed in a large iron pan along with vegetables and dumplings and boiled for many hours, thus producing a good nourishing soup. This operation was always spoken of as boiling't pot and the large iron pans used were named 'kale' pots. The dumplings were made from suet and flour with a little salt and generally eaten plain. At other times currants or fruit were added, making an extremely palatable and nourishing article of diet.

Salted beef and mutton were much used during the winter months, along with a little bacon by those who were fortunate enough to keep a pig.

There being no arable land in the higher reaches of Swaledale the custom was, prior to the middle of the last century, for the farmers and many of the miners to journey to Richmond to buy their wheat. At that date much corn was marketed in Richmond; generally the red corn. This was sold by the bole (140 lbs avoirdupois). After arranging with the farmers or miller as to quantity and price, arrangements were then made for the wheat to be milled as specified by the buyer.

A given percentage had to be made into white flour, wheaten flour, bran etc., sufficient for one year's home and farm supply. The bread made from this flour was often of a very poor quality, great difficulty being experienced in getting it to ferment and rise.

Yeast had to be obtained from the brewery carter who came from Kirkby Stephen. When the moorland roads were blocked with snow, baking was impossible.

Very few vegetables were grown in the dale and the supply necessary had to be imported from arable districts. Potatoes, turnips and apples were generally bought in sufficient quantities for the winter. Most of the people in the upper parts of the dale received their supplies of vegetables from Westmorland.

Fuel

The farmers bringing supplies from the arable districts generally came with two large cart loads of farm produce which they sold in their travels up the dale, their final destination being Tan Hill colliery or King's Pit,

Wash day at Muker. (S. Lee)

where they loaded with coal for the return journey; coals being 3d per cwt. Tan Hill Pit was a very important colliery and supplied a large area. Coal carts came to the pit from such distant places as Appleby and Northallerton.

Peat was also used as a household fuel by miners and farmers. All the houses in the Swaledale villages had turbary rights – the right to cut peat on the parish moor.

Water

All the villages received their water supply from the village pump, or springs nearby; none of the houses had a piped water supply. This necessitated carrying water, in many cases considerable distances. Consequently many cleansing operations were not very efficiently accomplished.

The sanitary arrangements in all the villages were of a very primitive type and, from a sanitary standpoint, chaos reigned. The privy cesspool system obtained in all the villages throughout the dale.

The old stone drains of the villages often became very offensive during periods of heat and drought in summer time, giving rise to many air borne diseases. Epidemic diseases such as typhus fever, typhoid fever, diphtheria and smallpox often ravaged the villages. The writer has often heard old people relate the sad story of these visitations, when almost every house in the village had lost one or more of its occupants, either adults or children.

Land

In addition to mining, many of the miners rented a small piece of land where they could keep a cow and perhaps a pig for household use. Whether this was a help to them or not seems questionable when we consider the high price they paid for their land – which was at least double the price paid per acre by the farmers of today – and the low price of farm produce; cheese being 2d to 4d per lb, with butter in summer at 6d per lb., perhaps reaching 1/- per pound in winter. These excessive rents were the result of competition amongst the miners for land. Whenever a small field was to let, many of them bid a higher rent, the result being rents soared upwards at every change of tenancy.

Knitting

To augment the miners' uncertain earnings many of their wives took in knitting which they performed in their spare time after attending to domestic duties. This knitting was let out by various hosiery firms from the large towns, who had agents in the dale. The price paid for handknitting men's long stockings was 2/- to 2/6 per dozen pairs. Fishermen's jerseys and thick wool stockings were also knit at very low rates of pay.

Knitting became a highly skilled trade amongst the housewives of the dale and the speed at which some of these ladies could knit had to be seen to be believed. In the operation they used short bent knitting needles and, around their waists, a leather strap which supported a knitting shear – a peculiar shaped piece of wood with a hole sunk deep at one end – as a receptable for one of the needles.

Placing an empty needle in the shear they began to knit and fill the empty needle with stitches or loops, at the same time making an upward and downward rhythmic movement of the hands as each loop was knit. This movement was called wapping. By this mode of knitting some of the most skilled women could knit a pair of men's long stockings from tea to suppertime. To save candlelight and fire they often went in turns to each other's houses having knitting nights.

Lighting

During the 18th century and the early years of the 19th the only means of illuminating the small miners' cottages was the rushlight. These were manufactured at home by the young members of the family. During summer time thick well grown rushes were procured. Whilst still moist the bark was cut longitudinally, the whole length of the rush, and the spongy pith bared by a thrust of the finger nail. The long prepared piths were dipped in hot melted tallow, then lifted out to harden in the air. After which, the operation was repeated again and again until they had acquired the requisite thickness.

Clothing

Clothing was intended to be serviceable rather than ornamental.

It was no uncommon sight to see miners wearing a pair of new corduroy or moleskin trousers at Church or Chapel on Sundays. Afterwards these saw service at the mine, to be replaced by new ones for Sunday. Clothing was made by local tailors, who made their living by travelling to the houses of miners and farmers. For their services they were paid 2/- to 2/6 per day along with their food. The cloth was generally bought from the several cloth peddlers who attended the local fairs held at almost all the Swaledale villages.

The ladies of the dale generally wore bonnets and wincey frocks. They had to be as thrifty and resourceful in their use as possible. After long usage bonnets were turned by the village milliner. The writer has an old account book belonging to one of the milliners; the maximum charge for turning a bonnet being one shilling and sixpence.

Relief

Frugality was often of no avail in warding off poverty. If a family became destitute and had no resources their only hope was to apply for poor law relief from the local overseers of the parish, who were often church-wardens appointed at the vestry meeting. Relief was distributed with extraordinary care and caution. Viewed from the present day standards it was wholly inadequate for the purpose for which it was intended. As a consequence, the lives of some of the more unfortunate members of the community must certainly have been one of great trial and tribulation.

A few cases of relief given, taken from the overseer's accounts of the year 1812, will give the reader some idea of the meagre help given to some of the unfortunate recipients.

Relieved: Bet Harper	1/-
John Clarkson (Lackey)	1/-
James Clarkson (Lackey)	1/-
Ells's daughter 4yd cotton 2yds for a shift	6/8
Bet Harper, Blue Woolen for a petticoat	5/6
Betty Carter, Muker 3 yeds Cotton @ 1/-	3/-
Paid Nanny Ell, gown and shirt making	1/-
Margaret Cooper, pair of clogs	2/11
Mary Cooper with	1/-
John Coaty's wife (Fidler) bought her a pair of blankets	11/-
Printed cotton for Bedgown	3/-
Cotton for lining it	1/8
John Coates doctor bill	10/-
Bought John Coates (Fidler) Clogs 1 pair 4/4)	
1 pair 2/- calkering (clog irons) 1/8 3/8)	8/-
Relieved James Clarkson Lackey	1/6

All recipients of poor law relief had their household goods confiscated and sold, with the exception of necessaries, by the overseers.

One of the sales of chattels prompted an old village poet, in Muker, to write the following verses.

"Lines written in consequence of that most infernal plot in the parish of Muker, made in order to deprive the paupers of all their furniture which the parish officers thought to be unnecessary and selling them by Public Auction on that most memorable day Muker Fair 1832"

Come all honest men who have sesses to pay
Let your care be attention to what I shall say
Your wise Vestry Laws restrictions and rules
Are left to a parcel of asses and fools.

Nay worse than all that, the intent upon evil
Their works proves that they are in league with the Devil
These human infernals, their masters surpass
In planning out evil, while drinking the glass.

Tis thought that Old Nick, when flying through't air
Alighted at Muker to peep round the fair
Poor Devil to view all the bustle and fun

And sure he might laugh, when he was outdone.

He passed through the people their manners to scan
Unseen, yet he whispered a devilish plan
That they should adopt, and with vigour pursue
Such measures none but an incarnate could do.

Yet who would have thought, it could enter the brains
As only such men as had hold of the reins
This business most surely, was hatched in hell
To take from the paupers their prayer books to sell.

Old Nick was pleased their tricks to behold
While gathering the trapsticks, or heaps to be sold
And Renny that sly fox, along with his cub
Seized hold of their prey, the poor people to rob.

These hard hearted monsters pursuing their plan
Seized their clocks sir, and cupboards, and the frying pan
Fire irons, hand irons, kitchen table and all
With various articles they made up the whole

Tis strange sir indeed that all these wiseacres
Themselves should demean, and so be partakers
Churchwardens, and members of Vestry combine,
To accomplish an object that was not Divine.

There are among them with horrid grimace
That will screw up his front, and grin in your face
He will boast of his riches, with long loud harangues
But trust me he has neither riches nor brains.

Did ere such a case as the present occur
All men in their senses must surely demur
None ever before this, beheld such a sight
Where the poor by the rich, were robbed of their right

Such sinners as these may shake hands and agree
To ease the poor people of their property
On Tommy they fix, as the most proper man
To bring to perfection, this horrible plan

On such an excursion, with two or three more
They did such an act, as was ne'er done before
Tis hoped such another, will not be again
So long as the parish of Muker remain.

In the year 1832, there was evidently great distress and a large number of paupers as the overseers were allowed a ½ rate distributed over the parish. This system continued until about the middle of the 19th century when a law was passed appointing Boards of Guardians.

The hard times then prevalent in the dale, and in many other districts of the British Isles, had one remarkable psychological effect; they steeled

Hay time at Thwaite. (B.L.)

Ruined peat store, old Gang Smelt Mill. (B.L.)

up every member of the community and made them give of their best in order to avoid destitution. Every effort was made by many of the miners to improve their financial position and augment their scanty earnings. After working hours at the mines many of them contracted to get peats on the adjoining moors, for use at the smelting mills where large quantities were used in smelting the ore. The cutters were paid 4d. per cart load.

After being dried on the moor during summer the peats were stored in large sheds near the smelting mills. A sufficient quantity had to be cutone year to last the whole of the following year. At some large mills thousands of cartloads were used every year.

Some miners broke limestones for the roads, their rate of pay being 1d. per bushel. The surveyor measured the stones to the quarter of a bushel and paid in farthings.

About the middle of the last century, 1840 to 1870, the commons in many parts of Swaledale were divided and enclosed. This necessitated building stone walls, liming and draining the land to improve cultivation. Much of this work was done by miners after working a shift at the mines. The small supplement to their wages was a great help.

At haymaking times many miners hired themselves for one month to the various local farmers, receiving in wages, if mowers, £4 to £6 per month in addition to their food.

Before the introduction of the mowing machine, all the grass had to be cut by hand. This made the employment of extra manual labour a necessity.

This change of occupation from the dark dismal mines to the fresh air and the sunny meadows was much appreciated and was looked upon as an annual holiday and a brief respite from their monotonous toil in the dark.

Employment of boys in the mines

Education was of a very elementary standard. At some of the village schools – such as Muker Endowed School, Gunnerside, Low Row and Reeth – where a schoolmaster was engaged, a fairly good elementary education was given to those children whose parents could afford to keep them there till thirteen or fourteen years of age.

Muker being an endowed school, the managers allowed a few of the poorest parents to send their children to school on free scholarships.

Unfortunately, most boys left school at about eight or ten years of age, to commence work in the mines before they had had time to absorb the 3 Rs. As a consequence a large proportion of the male population was illiterate, as evidenced in many old documents which are signed with a mark. In some documents over fifty per cent are signed with a mark.

The work of some of the boys consisted in blowing the 'windy king' – a machine for conveying air to badly ventilated workings in the mine.

This was a very gloomy occupation, as the boy was working alone in a dark dismal level. The miners would be labouring some considerable distance away.

Other boys were employed in some of the very narrow low galleries or levels, named 'durk drifts'. Their work consisted of hauling the ore and vein material from the men and depositing it into a hopper in one of the rises. All rises had the larger portion of the rise divided off as a receptacle or hopper for ore and vein debris which was afterwards withdrawn and transferred down the main level, by horses, to the dressings. The remaining 2ft 6ins of the rise was known as a 'climbing end' whereby the miners ascended up to their work by using the timber at the sides as a ladder.

The boys performing this work wore a sort of harness made to fit over their shoulders and attached by a swivel to a bucket which they dragged behind them on the gallery floor.

Markets

Two of the villages in Swaledale, Muker and Reeth, had a customary market held every week for one day where most of the miners and farmers made their purchases for the coming week.

On market days the villages were well patronised; farmers from all the surrounding districts arriving on horseback.

The stables were full to overflowing at the village inns. Several tradesmen had stalls in the market place where they vended such household goods as butcher's meat, cloth, drapery, provender, etc.

Market days were attended with great regularity by the farmers, the occasion being an opportunity to meet friends, to chat over business matters and dispose of any surplus farm produce to the various dealers who came to buy. On this day the village inns recorded a brisk trade; very few of the community being abstainers. The result was that many of them tarried over the glass, having a social evening till late at night; often taking on board a liberal consignment of refreshment. That many of the old farmers managed to reach their distant moorland homes without accident was perhaps due more to the sagacity of the horses than to the skill of their riders.

Fairs

The fairs held at Muker, Gunnerside and Reeth were looked forward to by all the countryside. Their origin was probably economic, or perhaps originally religious; but they were chiefly looked upon in those times as a relaxation to the year's hard labours and a day set apart for revelry and fun. They were also an occasion when farmers, cattle dealers, and local tradesmen settled up their yearly accounts; ready money being a rare commodity in those days.

At these times the village inns had their accommodation taxed to its utmost limits. In addition to refreshments, one of the local violinists was engaged to provide music for dancing in the largest room of the house. Here the youths and maidens danced the old country cross dances, handed down through many generations.

At Reeth and Thwaite Fairs, large numbers of sheep were on sale. Buyers came from the northern towns to buy stock for slaughter. Many farmers from southern counties purchased large numbers of sheep for breeding purposes. These fairs were the only means whereby the Swaledale farmers could dispose of their surplus stock of sheep. Today this is largely done through the many auction marts.

The excitement of a village fair is recorded in the dialect poem: Reeth Bartle Fair. ('Bartle' probably refers to Saint Bartholomew.)

This mworning as I went to wark,
I met Curly just cumman heam
He had on a new flannin sark
An he saw 'at I'd just gitten t'seam
"Whars ta been;" sed awd Curly ta me;
"I've been doon to Reeth Bartle Fair,"
"Swat te doon, mun, sex needles," sed he

"An tell us what seets te saw thar."
Wya, t'lads all ther best shun had put on
Ant' lasses donn'd all ther best cwoats,
I saw five pund o' Scotch wether mutton
Sell'd by Ward and Tish Tom for five grwoats
Bowlaway, lace an hankuchers browt;
Young Tom Cwoats hed a stall tury his-sel
An had ribbons for varra near nowt.

Thar was Enos had good brandy snaps
Bill Broon as good spices as cud be;
Potter Robin an mar syke – like chaps
Had t' bonniest pots te could see;
John Ridley an awd Willey Walls
An Naylor, an twea or three mar,
Had apples, an pears at ther stalls,
An Gardiner Joe teaa was thar.

Thar was sizzors an knives, an reaad pusses
An plenty of owd cleeathes o' t' nogs;
An tweea or three awd spavin'd hosses
An plenty of shun an new clogs,
Thar was plaenty of good iron pans,
An pigs 'at wad fill all t' deeal's hulls
Thar was baskets, an skeps, an tin cans,
An bowls, an wood thivels for gulls.

Thar was plenty of all macks o' meeat,
An plenty of all sworts o' drink;

An t' lasses gat monny a treat,
Forht' gruvers war all full o' chink.
I coup'd mi black hat for a white in;
Lile Jonas had varra cheap cleeath
Jem Peacock and Tom talk't o' feightin,
But Gudgeon Jem Puke licked em beeath.

Thar was dancin' an feightin for ever;
Will Wade sed 'at he was quite grieved,
An Pedelty tell'd em heed niver
Forgit am as lang as he lieved
They knock'd yan another aboot
Just wass than a sham to be seen
Charlie Will luked as white as a cloot
Kit Puke gat a pair o' black een.

I spied our awd lass in a nuke
Drinkan shrub wi grim Freesteeane, fond lad,
I gav her a varra grow luke,
O connies, but I was just mad.
Seea I went to John Whaites's to drink
Whar I war'd tweea an sevenpense i' gin
I knaw not what follow'd but think
I'd paddled through t' much thick an' thin.

For to day when I gat oot a bed,
My cleeas were all sullied sea sar;
Our Peggy an all our fwoak sed
To Reeth Fair I sud never ga mar;
But its rake-time, sea I mun away
For my partners are all g'yan to work;
Seea I lowp't up an bad him good day
An wrowt at t'Awd Gang till it was dark.

swat – squat
six needles – a phrase signifying an interval of time during which a woman knitting would work the 'loops' of six needles

wya – well
shun – shoes
handkitchers – handkerchiefs
brandy snaps – ginger biscuits
lowpt – jumped
spice – gingerbread
nogs – wooden pegs
gruvers – miners
chink – money
cowp't – exchanged
Puke – surname Peacock
twea an sevenpence – 2/7
Awd Gang – name of lead mine
Shrub – a liqueur
hulls – pig stys
rake-time – mine time

Few people were known by their proper names, almost all of them had a by-name by which they were identified.

During the threatened invasion of England by Bonaparte about the year 1804, volunteer corps were raised in Swaledale, and stationed at Richmond, under the command of Captain Metcalfe. In the muster rolls of the Dales volunteers were the following names:

Thos Alderson Grain Tom
" Glowermore Tom
" Screamer Tom
" Poddish Tom
" Tarry Tom
" Tish Tom
" Tripy Tom
" Trooper Tom
Butter Geordie
Bullock Jemmie
Buck Reuben
Becks Jack
Bullet
Brag Tom
Angry Jack
Assy Will Bill
Aysgill Tom Bill
Docken Jammie
Kit Puke Jock
Kanah Bill
Knocky Gwordie
Nettlebed Anty
Peter Tom Willy
Peed Jack
Piper Ralph
Shodder
Splitmeat
Swinny
Tazzy Will

Dant
Freestone Jack
Gudgeon Tom
Hed Jack
John Hird Awd John
" Young John
" Jains Jack
" Mary Jack
" King Jack
Katey Tom Elick
Kanah Bell
Knock Gwordie
Piper Ralph
Pullan Will
Roberty Will Peg Sam
Rive Rags
Curly
Dickey Tom Johnny
Bowlaway
Brownsea Jossy
Cis Will
Cotty Joe
Codgy
Cweaty Jack
Slipe
Skeb Symy
Sturgeon Will
Tash

Here we see eight Aldersons with nick-names and five Hirds.

Superstitions

The miners were very superstitious. If they discovered ore, on no account would they touch the ore with their picks, but would work as far as they could forward on each side of the ore, the idea being the further they could work on each side, the surer the continuity of the ore and its greater mass.

Another unforgivable sin in the mine was for any of the miners to whistle; the shrill sound was supposed to make the ore vanish, never to reappear. It was always bad luck for a tailor to go into or near one of the mines and if one did so it was at his peril as he was sure of either a good thrashing or a severe reprimand.

River Swale at Wain Wath Force. (B.L.)

Although Swaledale is an agricultural district the conversation in the villages, and especially the village inns, was chiefly on mining. The miners, having a numerical advantage over the farmers, monopolised the conversation, spinning their yarns about the rich mines they knew of. Many were the records handed down from father to son of the rich deposits of ore which had been left unworked by the old man because of flooding. It was on these occasions, when the imagination was excited by strong liquers, that the miner described his 'El Dorado' which nearly everyone fancied to exist in some chosen spot – usually unattainable because of water trouble or the hesitation of the lessees to explore the fancied region of riches.

This element in the miner's character gave an exhilaration to his calling as he always felt he might be on the verge of riches which would lift him from the precariousness of poverty. Often trials were made of the land of promise, but as the gloomy recesses of the mountain were explored, the fairy vision failed to materialise.

Sporting

During leisure hours the miners were keen sportsmen, and Swaledale with its rivers and moors – refuges for many kinds of game – was there to be exploited. As a consequence many of the miners availed themselves of these opportunities for recreation and, more important, the procuring of a little free food.

The rivers were well stocked with trout and free to the whole community; the Lord of the Manor allowing all residents to fish free. Hence many of them spent several happy hours at the riverside in a sport whose chief feature was expectancy; not unlike their calling in the mines. In flood times the still pools near the river's bank were swept with cowl nets and large quantities of trout secured.

Ground game, such as rabbits and hares, were protected by the Game Laws as also were the grouse and birds on the adjoining moors. These were closely watched by a number of gamekeepers. But the miners were often keen poachers, looking on the game preserves as the wild gift of nature and the heritage of all.

Hares were abundant in Swaledale up to the passing of the Ground Game Act. Afterwards nearly all farmers procured a gun and today hares are scarce. If snow fell, making it easy to trace the hares by their footmarks, many of the miners took it as an opportunity for having a night's poaching with dogs and nets.

The grouse on the surrounding moors did not escape the miners' attention. The more daring of them – often in gangs – went poaching on the moors, shooting or netting the grouse by night. The nets used were large ones, perhaps 50 yards square. These were dragged over the heather. As the sleeping grouse were startled into flight the men dropped the net, imprisoning the birds.

To prevent poaching many parts of the moors were studded with poles and bushes as an impediment to the dragging of nets.

One poaching story has been handed down from the mining times. The chief protagonists were the noted old gamekeeper Cherry Kearton – grandfather to the late Richard Kearton, F.Z.S., the naturalist – and a young man who lived on a farmstead near the village of Ivelet. The old gamekeeper had a rude stone refuge built on the moor from which point of vantage he could survey a considerable area of heather clad hill. This refuge still stands and today is named Cherr Currock.

Towards dusk one evening the old gamekeeper espied a man in the distance. A short time afterwards he heard the report of a gun which had been fired at a grouse he had disturbed. As quickly as possible, the old gamekeeper started off in pursuit of the poacher whom he soon recognised as a young miner living at one of the farms on the hillside below. The young man, seeing the gamekeeper in the distance running towards him, made off home as quickly as possible. Arriving home breathless with exertion he hurriedly hid the grouse, procured a saw and climbed up one of the large trees near the farm, starting at once to saw off one of the branches.

Shortly afterwards the old gamekeeper arrived on the scene and saw the young man up the tree unconcernedly sawing off one of the branches.

He shouted to the young man, "Thou's been on t' moor shutan. I've seen tha." There was no response. The miner, pretending not to hear him, proceeded with his work.

Using nets the miners poached grouse on the moors. (Carole Pugh)

To the surprise of the old gamekeeper there was a sudden crack and the branch, with the miner still astride it, was deposited at his feet. In his haste to saw through the branch the young man had carelessly sat on the wrong side of the saw cut. The old gamekeeper, a noted local preacher and kindhearted man, assisted the young man to his feet and, after enquiring if he was hurt, wended his way home, happy to think that a divine providence had intervened with a chastisement that no sinner could escape. Perhaps he also gave thanks to the Lord that he himself had been spared the irksome task of administering justice.

In the early part of the nineteenth century the Weardale miners came on poaching expeditions into Swaledale and gave the local gamekeepers a considerable amount of trouble. One party which often came was led by a fine specimen of a man named Paul Armstrong, a strong robust miner. Each man of the party had a gun and a large savage dog. All of them seem to have been men of a callous combative temperament. The gamekeepers and farmers were much afraid of them and they were known in the neighbourhood as the 'Wardil Warriors'. On one of their occasional visits they shot the old gamekeeper, Cherry Kearton, in the legs; for which act came later retribution.

Keeping his vigil one evening on the moor, the alert eye of the old gamekeeper espied them in the distance. He at once went to a hiding place to further observe their movements. They passed him without discovery and he followed them at a distance till nightfall, when he observed them go into a cowhouse near the Kirkby Stephen road. At once he went round to the dalehead farms for help to capture them in their lair. He collected ten farmers with guns who went and surrounded the cowhouse during the night.

At sunrise Paul Armstrong appeared and looking out said to his men, "It's a fine morning, we must be off." Instantly the ten farmers appeared from their hiding places.

Armstrong was furious, declaring that the first man who went near would be shot. In the meantime, some of the men had drawn nearer the cowhouse. Armstrong and his men decided to rush and risk it but he was knocked down with the butt end of a gun by one of the farmers. The gang were all taken prisoner, and their fate decided at Richmond police court.

A pack of hounds was always kept in the dale, chiefly for hare hunting. The day arranged for a meet of the hounds was looked forward to by many of the miners who made it a general holiday which was spent following the hounds. It was common practice to keep a hound which could be liberated to join the pack whenever the horn of the hutsman was heard.

The hilly nature of the country-side helped greatly in making the hare hunting interesting. Good vantage points could be found affording a view over a wide expanse of country. This made it possible for the spectators to keep in view both hare and hounds for long distances. Many of the younger men followed the hounds on foot. Some of these hunts were an inspiration to the dale's poets who wrote and set to music several fine local hunting songs.

Over one hundred years ago, a very important local hound trail meeting was held every year at Tan Hill, where hounds from the surrounding localities of Wensleydale, Arkengarthdale, Swaledale, and Westmorland met to compete.

Before hound trails a man set off dragging behind him a piece of sacking which had been scented with aniseed. After a tortuous journey of several miles over the fells he returned to the starting point. The hounds were then released and, picking up the scent, away they went following the track made by the man. The winner was the hound which completed the course first.

The Tan Hill meeting always drew large crowds of spectators. It was the setting for many a celebrated run. One, in particular, is worthy of mention.

Two miners from the hamlet of Low Row had entered their hounds for the Tan Hill trail. On the day of the competition the two miners rose early. The morning being fine, they decided to take a short route over the moors to Tan Hill. Their route led them to the top of Gunnerside Gill. When they reached Blakethwaite lead mine they decided it was time for a short rest and a pipe of tobacco. Scarcely had they sat down when, to their surprise, up sprang a fine fox from some rushes near the mine dam.

Making an instant decision, one of the miners exclaimed, "Slip the dog, Jack." Jack complied with alacrity. The hound set off, hard on the heels of

A memorable chase. (Carole Pugh)

his quarry. When the miner saw his dog had gone he said to his friend, "Thee slip thine."

Immediately, the other hound set off in pursuit of the fox and had soon disappeared from sight. The miners waited anxiously, expecting their dogs to return. Their wait was in vain so the miners continued their journey to Tan Hill, dejected at the loss of their dogs and the missed opportunity of entering the hound trail.

When they arrived at Tan Hill they decided to drown their sorrows in one of the three alehouses. (Now, only one remains.) After a few hours worship at the 'shrine of Bachus' they became quarrelsome, one saying to the other, "If it hadn't been for thee I shouldn't a slipt my dog." To which the other retorted, "An thoo tell'd me to slip mine." The result of this wrangle was a fight.

Towards evening, having become friends again, they started off over the moors for home. They were hopeful that their dogs would be waiting to greet them. Their hopes failed to materialize – the dogs were still missing.

At last, after four days of waiting, two very exhausted dogs returned. On examining the hounds the miners noticed a small roll of paper had been attached to the collar of each.

The notes had been fastened to the collars of the hounds by a gamekeeper in Northumberland – near the Scottish border – who had witnessed the dogs kill their quarry. The dogs were in such a weak state that he took them to his kennels and fed them for several days prior to their release on the morning of the fourth day.

To commemorate such a feat of tenacity and endurance, one of the lead smelters at Old Gang lead mines moulded two lead dogs which were erected – with great liquid rejoicings – over the sign of the Punch Bowl Hotel, Low Row. There they remained till the rebuilding of the hotel. Unfortunately they were destroyed during the alterations, none of the workmen knowing their historic value.

Religion

The introduction of Wesleyan Methodism, about the year 1750, had a remarkable influence on the subsequent history of Swaledale.

The great revival of spiritual emotion it excited in the minds of the mining population marks its incidence as one of the greatest events for the improvement of the moral and spiritual welfare of the people.

Prior to the introduction of methodism the spiritual needs of the dale had been under the auspices of the two Established Churches of Grinton and Muker; with the exception of several small meeting houses in the villages where a few Quakers and nonconformists worshipped. After the passing of the Conformity Laws many of them were tried at York assizes for non-attendance at divine worship. At this date the 'Good Lord Wharton' sheltered many ministers who had been expelled from their churches under the Conformity Laws. Tradition relates that non-conformists had to meet secretly in Swinnergill Kirk – a small cave on the wild moorlands – and there worship unseen by their prying neighbours who were ever ready to inform and receive half the fine imposed on their victims.

Soon after the passing of the 'Five Mile Act' allowing dissenting places of worship to be built at that distance from an established church the 'Good Lord Wharton' erected for the use of his miners in the 17th century a small chapel at Smarber, near Low Row.

John Wesley paid several visits to Swaledale, his first in 1761. On his arrival at Low Row he found a society whose conduct he greatly commended. In his journal for 1768, Wesley records the community of Low Row as being: "One of the most lively which I have met with in England." In another part of his journal he writes: "I have not found so deep and lively a work in any other part of the Kingdom as runs through the whole circuit, particularly in the vales which wind through these horrid mountains."

The Wesleyan Chapels at Low Row, Muker, Gunnerside, Arkengarthdale and Keld, as well as many others in the dale, were built chiefly by the miners who did most of the preliminary work such as the cutting of foundations and the quarrying of stone. After building the chapels, many of the miners developed a great yearning to improve themselves intellectually, the result being the building in many of the villages of small literary institutes and libraries. These edifices were used as public meeting places for lectures etc.; also as places for entertainment where local

Muker Institute. (S. Lee)

concerts were held and 'penny readings' which went some way towards relieving the monotony of village life. During most of the evenings the institutes were full of men learning to read and write; the teachers being miners who were somewhat better educated than their less fortunate friends.

Changes

In the last quarter of the 19th century the Swaledale lead trade began to decline. The price of lead fell from over £20 a ton to £8 and £9 a ton. Many of the mines could no longer be worked at a profit and several companies were forced into liquidation.

These unfortunate economic circumstances were brought about by the importation into Britain of large quantities of lead ore from Spain where some valuable and rich lead mines had been discovered at Rio Tinto. The ore contained a high percentage of silver which was of sufficient value to pay for the working of the mines. Hence the lead was looked upon almost as a by product and sold cheaply in the English lead markets.

Tramp steamers often called at Spanish ports to ballast their holds with lead ore which they brought to England at a ridiculously low rate. This deplorable economic upheaval which befell the Swaledale lead trade brought, as a consequence, many changes in the social and economic life of the dale.

The miners, seeing their only livelihood had vanished, and nothing but starvation staring them in the face, had to seek work elsewhere. From the upper reaches of the dale a few pioneers set out to find work in the Lancashire coal mines at Burnley and in the surrounding districts. Having found work in the coal mines, and their children work in the cotton factories, they wrote home to their friends in Swaledale telling them their good fortune and inviting them to come, as they had already made arrangements for them to start work on their arrival.

At the lower end of the dale in Gunnerside, Low Row and Reeth, most of the miners and their families migrated into the county of Durham to work at the coal mines there. It is recorded that as many as forty families went into Lancashire during one winter. Swaledale names are very common in Lancashire and Durham mining districts.

In many cases the disaster was turned to advantage. Work was plentiful and well paid in both Lancashire and Durham when compared to the scanty earnings they had been accustomed to in the lead mines of Swaledale. No difficulty was experienced in finding work in the cotton mills and factories of Lancashire. As a consequence many of them soon became much better off than they had ever been. Yet, with all their good fortune their minds would often wander to Swaledale, where they again in fancy relived the days of their youth. Many of them were never to return to their villages until, at their death, they were brought back to be buried in their native dale; re-united with the sights and sounds of their youth.

Glossary of mining terms

Bucker: A flat faced iron mallet used to crush stones in which lead is disseminated.
Beater: An iron chisel with blunt semi circular end used to pack bore holes, when blasting, to confine the explosive.
Bearing barrow: Wooden box with handles at each end, used by miners in odd places to carry their work to the wagon.
Bulling: A term used during blasting operations when gunpowder was used as the only explosive. Occasionally a hole bored into the rock tapped a small amount of water. Consequently the powder, when inserted, would have been damped and its explosive properties impaired. To obviate this, a tallow candle was inserted after removal of the wick and a ramrod inserted to press the tallow into any crevice. Thus the hole was made watertight. This was termed by miners 'bulling the hole'. If the above process was not adopted, thick grease-proof, brown paper was used and a rude powder cartridge made.
Clevis: A large blacksmith-made swivel for attaching to the end of a rope, into which fitted the handle of a large wooden bucket called a kibble, used for drawing the ore from a shaft.
Cowlrake: A tool used by miners much the shape of a garden hoe; used for raking the ore and stones together during the process of dressing.
Fuse: Used in blasting operations to ignite the powder, gelignite, or other explosive material. About the thickness of a small lead pencil and the powder in the centre of the fuse is exactly the same as the lead running down the centre of the pencil. The powder used in the fuse burns very slowly to allow the miners time to get to a place of safety after lighting it.
Jumper: A long chisel used by miners for boring the rock for blasting purposes. These jumpers were made of about 1 inch square wrought iron, with a piece of shear steel welded on one end to form the cutting edge.

Jumpers were used during the whole period of mining in Swaledale, after the introuction of explosives, and old miners preferred them to the new all steel ones. The shot holesbored by the miners varied from about 18 inches to 2 feet, according to the rock and explosive used.
Kibble: A wooden bucket used for drawing up stones and ore from shafts and sumps. In engine shafts the kibble was often made of wrought iron.
Launder: A wooden trough used much in mines for conducting water.
Limp: A wooden instrument about 15 inches wide and 7 inches deep sheathed with iron, used to scrape off small stones from the seieve during sotching; one of the processes used in dressing the ore and ridding it of stones and clay.
Needle: Long needle shaped piece of copper about one-third of an inch in diameter, used for keeping a small hole open for the introduction of the squib or fuse by which the gunpowder is exploded in blasting operations. In the early days of mining, these needles were made of iron or steel which resulted in many serious accidents due to a spark resulting from friction

against the hard rock – the result being the copper needle was made compulsory by Act of Parliament.

Scraper: Tool made of thin rod iron used in boring in the rock to scrape out bore hole dust made by the cutting of the rock.

Stemming: The process of filling and packing tight with stone the hole made for blasting to confine the powder. This was accomplished by an iron chisel much the same as the jumper but thinner, with a semicircular blunt end called a 'beater'.

Squib: A long narrow piece of paper into which has been sprinkled powder and then wrapped up longitudinally much the same as we make a paper spill or lighter. These were used in blasting operations, and introduced into the hole made by the needle, and thrust down to make contact with the powder. When the miner had done this, he took another piece of paper, which he covered with the tallow from his candle, and screwed the paper up into a roll about 3 inches long. One end of this paper he thrust into a piece of clay, and by that means stuck it on to the rock at right angles to the squib, which was near the clay end. The miner then lighted one end, and during the time this was burning he retired to a place of safety before the explosion. Touch paper was also used, this being brown paper soaked in a strong solution of saltpetre. This paper smoulders away very slowly, and a piece of this was introduced into the end of the squib and lighted. Fuse began to be used in the Swaledale Mines after the introduction of guncotton, dynamite and gelignite. In the process of blasting after boring the hole in the rock, a given quantity of blasting powder – this being large grained powder – was introduced and thrust to the bottom. The needle was then introduced and the paper thrust down around the needle to form a wad. Then stone and plate were hammered down by the 'beater' until the hole was full. The needle was then withdrawn and the squib inserted to make contact with the powder. The explosive was by these means confined and made capable of doing its work.